YOU CHOOSE

ANCIENT GREECE

An Interactive History Adventure

by William Caper

Consultant:
Jonathan M. Hall
Phyllis Fay Horton Distinguished Service Professor
in the Humanities
Professor and Chair, Department of Classics
Professor, Department of History and the College
The University of Chicago

Raintree is an imprint of Capstone Global Library Limited, a company incorporated in England and Wales having its registered office at 7 Pilgrim Street, London, EC4V 6LB – Registered company number: 6695582

www.raintreepublishers.co.uk
myorders@raintreepublishers.co.uk

ISBN 978 1 474 70647 6
19 18 17 16 15
10 9 8 7 6 5 4 3 2 1

Printed and bound in China

British Library Cataloguing in Publication Data
A full catalogue record for this book is available from the British Library.

Photo Credits
akg-images: 92, Peter Connolly, 78, 89; The Art Archive: NGS Image Collection/H.M. Herget, 6, 16, 35, 51, 53, 73, 83; The Bridgeman Art Library International: ©Look and Learn/Private Collection, 67; ©Look and Learn/Private Collection/Harry Green, 12; ©Look and Learn/Private Collection/Howat, Andrew, 102; ©Look and Learn/Private Collection/Payne, Roger, cover, 43, 56; ©Look and Learn/Private Collection/Uptton, Clive, 45; Archives Charmet/Private Collection, 36; Private Collection/Burton, H. M., 26; Private Collection/Heath, Dudley, 40; Private Collection/Weatherstone, A. C., 81; Capstone: Compass Point Books/Chris Forsey, 68; Corbis: PoodlesRock, 33; The Image Works: Photo12, 29; Johnny Shumate, 21; Mary Evans Picture Library: Edwin Wallace, 98; North Wind Picture Archives: 14, 60, 62, 85

Every effort has been made to contact copyright holders of material reproduced in this book. Any omissions will be rectified in subsequent printings if notice is given to the publisher.

All the internet addresses (URLs) given in this book were valid at the time of going to press. However, due to the dynamic nature of the internet, some addresses may have changed, or sites may have changed or ceased to exist since publication. While the author and publisher regret any inconvenience this may cause readers, no responsibility for any such changes can be accepted by either the author or the publisher.

TABLE OF CONTENTS

About your ADVENTURE

YOU are living in ancient Greece. It's a time of great advances in society. But there's also the threat of war and danger. What will happen to you?

In this book, you'll explore how the choices people made meant the difference between life and death. The events you'll experience happened to real people.

Chapter one sets the scene. Then you choose which path to read. Follow the directions at the bottom of each page. The choices you make will change your outcome. After you finish one path, go back and read the others for new perspectives and more adventures.

YOU CHOOSE the path
you take through history.

The ancient Greeks gathered in public for weddings and other celebrations.

A CULTURED CIVILIZATION

Greece was the birthplace of western civilization. During the 500s BC, Greek thinkers established the principles of science and philosophy. Greek leaders gave the world the beginnings of democracy. People still admire the art and architecture of ancient Greece and read stories about its gods and goddesses.

Ancient Greece was never a united nation. Instead, it was made up of more than 1,500 city-states. A city-state was made up of a city or town, plus the surrounding villages and land. Each city-state had its own government. But a common language, religion, and culture tied the Greeks together.

Turn the page.

The most powerful city-states were Athens and Sparta. Athens had the biggest Greek navy. Athens controlled a part of Greece called Attica and led a group of about 200 city-states called the Delian League. The city-states in the league paid money to Athens in return for protection. This tribute made Athens rich.

Sparta had the most powerful Greek land army. Sparta controlled a part of Greece called Laconia and had its own alliance, the Peloponnesian League. The city-states in the league didn't have to send money to Sparta. But they did have to supply Sparta with soldiers in times of war.

Athenians and Spartans lived very different lives. Athenians prided themselves on developing art, culture, and science. People today still read the works of playwright Sophocles and philosopher Plato.

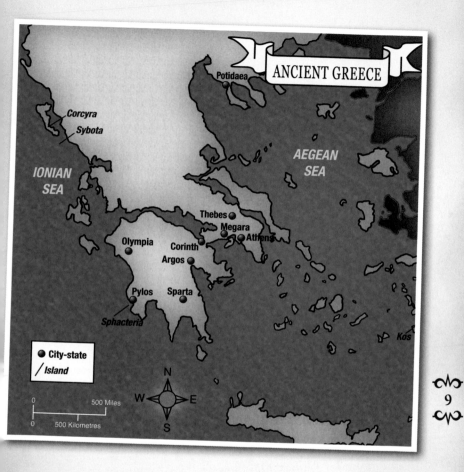

ANCIENT GREECE

Potidaea

Corcyra
Sybota

IONIAN
SEA

AEGEAN
SEA

Thebes
Megara
Athens
Olympia
Corinth
Argos

Pylos
Sparta

Sphacteria

Kos

● City-state
/ Island

N
W ◆ E
S

0   500 Miles
0   500 Kilometres

Turn the page.

Athenian culture reached its height during a period that lasted from about 461 to 404 BC. This time is called the Golden Age of Athens. During this period, Athens thrived. Its citizens enjoyed luxuries and foods from all over Greece.

Sparta was at its height during a period that lasted from about 550 to 371 BC. In Sparta, luxury wasn't important. Spartan citizens weren't allowed to own gold or silver. Spartans focused on serving the state. At age 7, boys were taken from their parents and sent to military schools. They learned to live under harsh conditions and stern discipline.

Women also had different roles in Athens and Sparta. In Athens, women and girls weren't educated. Wealthy women seldom left their homes. Spartan girls were educated and were treated as equals to boys. They learned to fight but did not become soldiers.

The era of ancient Greece was a time of discovery and learning. What will you experience as you travel there?

• To see what life was like in Athens during the 400s BC, turn to page **13**.

• To see what life was like in Sparta during the 400s BC, turn to page **63**.

People of Athens gathered on the steps of the Parthenon to discuss the issues of the day.

CHAPTER 2

CITY OF WISDOM

You are a citizen of Athens. One morning, you take a walk through the busy city. You pass three types of people – citizens, noncitizens, and slaves. Citizens are people like you who were born in Athens. They include farmers, wealthy aristocrats, and craftspeople. You see few aristocratic women. Women and girls of this class stay at home. They are considered the property of their husbands. Women can be citizens, but they have no political rights.

Noncitizens include people who came from outside Athens. They can't own land, but they can own businesses or work in industry. Slaves make up the lowest class of people. They have no rights.

13

Turn the page.

Aristocratic women
supervised the work
of the household.

You cross the acropolis. Some of Athens' most important buildings stand on this protected hill. One building, the Parthenon, is an enormous temple honouring Athena, the goddess of wisdom. The city is named for her.

You keep walking and arrive at the Pnyx, the hill where the Assembly meets. Members of the Assembly decide important issues that affect the city, including whether or not to go to war.

Soon you reach the agora. This open area serves as a place for trade and meetings. The agora is also where trials are held and law cases are heard.

Everywhere you go, the city bustles with activity. This is a good time to be a citizen of Athens. There are many things to do, many things to enjoy, and many ways to live your life.

‣ *To be a government official, turn to page* **16**.

‣ *To be a sculptor, turn to page* **30**.

‣ *To be a philosopher or a doctor, turn to page* **40**.

Unlike girls, boys in Athens attended school.

You grew up in an aristocratic family in Athens. You attended a local school as a child. Your parents then hired a private teacher called a sophist to teach you mathematics, geography, science, and philosophy. At age 18, you were considered a citizen. After serving two years in the army, you took your place in the Assembly.

Now, at age 30, you are married and own a large house and several slaves. Best of all, you are a friend and adviser to Pericles. Pericles has led Athens for 29 years.

Under Pericles' leadership, Athens has become wealthy and powerful. Athens and Sparta have spent the last 30 years mostly at peace. But now, in 432 BC, conflict is growing. People in both cities are talking of war.

One night, you have supper with Pericles at his house. You dine on fish, lentils, pomegranates, and figs as you sip wine mixed with water. Drinking wine at full strength is considered bad manners. For dessert, a servant girl brings delicious honey cakes.

After supper, you and Pericles go into the courtyard to talk. He tells you, "The city-state Corcyra is at war with Corinth and has asked us for help. Corinth is an ally of Sparta. Helping Corcyra will increase the risk of war between Athens and Sparta. But Athens can't avoid war with Sparta, and I want Corcyra as an ally."

Turn the page.

"Why is Corcyra so important?" you ask.

"The size of its navy is second only to that of Athens," Pericles replies. "Plus, its location on the Ionian Sea will give us an important naval base. I'm sending 10 ships to Corcyra, and I want you to go with them. Our soldiers have orders not to fight unless the Corinthians try to land on Corcyra."

18

· To go to Corcyra, go to page **19**.

· To refuse, turn to page **24**.

You've agreed to help Pericles. You are now standing on the deck of a ship off the Sybota islands near Corcyra. Your hand rests on your sword, but you won't fight unless you are directly attacked. You are here only as Pericles' observer.

The ships of Athens and Corcyra are facing ships from Corinth and one of its allies, Megara. All the ships carry archers and heavily armed soldiers called hoplites.

After furious fighting on both sides, some enemy ships retreat. Some Corcyraean ships leave the battle to chase the retreating enemy ships. But with these ships gone, the Corcyraean fleet is weaker. Spears and arrows fill the air as the Corinthians sink many Corcyraean ships. Corinthian soldiers board their enemies' ships, killing soldiers and taking prisoners.

Turn the page.

"The Corinthians are gaining the upper hand!" your captain shouts. "We must return to Corcyra to stop them from landing!"

The Athenian and Corcyraean captains turn their ships around and sail back to Corcyra. There the ships line up to prepare for another attack. You watch tensely as the enemy ships come closer.

But suddenly the Corinthians stop. Then they begin to back away. "The Corinthians are leaving!" a soldier yells. "Twenty more Athenian ships are here, and more are on the way!" There's no time to celebrate, though. You know that the Corinthians may return with more ships.

The next day, your ships are lined up again, in case the Corinthians try to land on Corcyra. Sure enough, the Corinthians return. But at the sight of your force, they turn around and sail away.

Athenian hoplites (left) fought alongside Corcyraeans at the Battle of Sybota.

As you watch the Corinthians leave, your captain appears at your side. "We've won a great victory," he says with a proud smile.

But you aren't so sure. The Corinthians didn't take Corcyra, but Corcyra still suffered heavy losses. "I think both sides will say they won this battle," you tell him.

The captain's smile fades. "What will you tell Pericles?" he asks.

· To tell Pericles that Athens won, turn to page **22**.

· To tell Pericles that Corinth won, turn to page **23**.

"Sybota was an Athenian victory," you tell Pericles when you return home. "The Corinthians were stopped from landing on Corcyra. The next day, they retreated."

Pericles is pleased. He says, "I'm taking action against two other allies of Corinth, Megara and Potidaea. I've issued the Megarian Decree. This order will stop Megara from trading with Athens and the rest of the Delian League. Also, I'm sending soldiers to march on Potidaea. The people there are upset that we've more than doubled the tribute they pay us. Now Corinth is encouraging Potidaea to rebel against Athens. I want you to go to Potidaea as my representative."

But you're not sure that action against Spartan allies is a good idea. What will you tell Pericles?

· To refuse to go to Potidaea, turn to page **24**.

· To go to Potidaea, turn to page **25**.

22

"Sybota was a Corinthian victory," you tell Pericles. "They sank almost 70 Corcyraean ships and took about 1,000 prisoners."

"But the Corinthians were stopped from landing on Corcyra!" Pericles replies angrily. "And they retreated the next day! Should I be questioning your loyalty to Athens?"

"Of course I'm loyal to Athens!" you reply, growing angry yourself. Your friendship with Pericles is becoming strained.

"There's a problem with Potidaea," Pericles continues. "Potidaea is a member of the Delian League and pays tribute to Athens. But I think the Corinthians are encouraging Potidaea to revolt. I'm sending soldiers to stop Potidaea from rebelling. I want you to go with them as my observer."

• To refuse to go to Potidaea, turn to page **24**.

• To go to Potidaea, turn to page **25**.

"I'm sorry," you tell Pericles, "but I can't go, either to fight or as your observer. I don't think we should seek war with Sparta. This is one of the best times in our history. Why risk all that?"

"We can't avoid war with Sparta," Pericles repeats. "As a citizen, it's your duty to support your city."

Pericles is set on fighting Sparta. If you continue to oppose him, you will lose a friend and gain a powerful enemy. But saving Athens from war might be more important than having Pericles as a friend.

24

Turn to page 29.

You are with the Athenian army at Potidaea. The Potidaeans have revolted against Athens, and Corinth has sent soldiers to help them. A battle has begun outside the city, and you are watching it from a hill.

In one part of the battle, the Corinthian troops overcome the Athenian soldiers. But overall, the Athenian soldiers win. At the end of the battle, the Corinthians and Potidaeans have lost about 300 men. Athens lost only about 150 soldiers.

After the battle, you congratulate one of the Athenian commanders. "This was only the first step," he tells you. "Now we're going to lay siege to Potidaea. If we stop food and supplies from getting into the city, the people will have no choice but to surrender completely. We could use your help. Can you stay here awhile?"

Turn the page.

Athenian soldiers
surrounded the walls of
Potidaea during the siege.

Pericles expects you to return to Athens

and report to him on the battle. But with the
problems in your friendship, you're not sure that
you want to do that. Maybe you should stay.

• To stay in Potidaea, go to page **27**.

• To return to Athens, turn to page **28**.

You stay in Potidaea to help plan the siege. At first everything goes well. Athenian soldiers surround the city, preventing supplies from reaching the people inside. Soon the Potidaeans are starving. They will soon have to give up.

One morning, a soldier rushes into your room. "There's something wrong with some of the men!" he shouts. "Please, come quickly!"

You follow him to the barracks. You are horrified by what you see. Some soldiers are bleeding from their mouths. Others are doubled over, vomiting onto the floor. You realize what's wrong. These soldiers have the plague!

You know that you should stay and try to help, but the plague is passed from one person to another. The best thing may be to flee to Athens while you're still well.

· To stay in Potidaea, turn to page **48**.

· To flee to Athens, turn to page **49**.

Back in Athens, you meet with Pericles. You're worried about the siege. With Corinth's support, the siege will be long and expensive for Athens.

"You should end the siege and bring back our troops," you tell Pericles.

"No," he responds. "I will continue the siege until Potidaea is taken."

You try again. "The Peloponnesian League is meeting in Sparta. The Corinthians and Potidaeans are asking Sparta to declare war on us. If we pull back now, I think we can avoid war."

"I don't care about that meeting!" Pericles sneers. "And our own allies will help us fight Sparta. Soon the Assembly will vote on war with Sparta. If you stand against me in the Assembly, our friendship is over!"

A speaker's platform and steps were carved into the Pnyx (right).

Days later, you go to the Pnyx for the Assembly meeting. Pericles stands on the platform, in the middle of a speech.

"The Spartans have made demands," Pericles says. "They want the Megarian Decree revoked. That will allow Megara to trade with Athens and the city-states in the Delian League. They also want us to end the siege of Potidaea. We must not give in to these demands. If we appear weak, other city-states will revolt against us. I call for a vote on war!"

· To vote against war, turn to page **50**.

· To vote for war, turn to page **52**.

Growing up in Athens, you were interested in many subjects. Careers in philosophy, medicine, and art all appealed to you. Your interest in art won out, and you became a student of Phidias. He is one of the most famous sculptors in Athens. Phidias is a close friend of Pericles, who has led Athens for the last 29 years.

About 50 years ago, the Persians attacked and destroyed much of Athens. Now that Athens is doing well, Pericles is rebuilding the city. Phidias is overseeing much of the construction. One day, you are working on a small statue in Phidias' workshop. You look up to see Phidias at your side.

"You are a hard worker and a good student," he says with a smile. "I've been watching you, and I think you have a great deal of talent."

These words make you proud, but what Phidias says next makes your heart soar. "I have two important projects. I'd like you to help me with one of them. One project is a building in Athens. The other is a statue. Which one would you rather work on?"

• To help Phidias with a building, turn to page **32**.

• To help Phidias with a statue, turn to page **34**.

You and Phidias stand before the Propylaea, the huge gateway to the acropolis. Phidias tells you, "This building was started about five years ago. There is still much work to be done on it."

Across the acropolis is the Parthenon. Work on this enormous marble temple started about 15 years ago. Inside the Parthenon is Phidias' huge new statue of Athena.

"The Parthenon will be finished later this year," Phidias says. "I think it will be one of Athens' most famous buildings."

After you and Phidias have studied both buildings, he offers you a choice. "Would you like to help finish the Parthenon? Or would you rather work on the Propylaea?"

· To help complete the Parthenon, go to page **33**.
· To work on the Propylaea, turn to page **53**.

Detailed sculptures covered the sides of the Parthenon's roof.

You decide to work on the Parthenon. This grand temple is dedicated to the goddess Athena. You help carve sculptures on the east and west ends of the roof. These sculptures show important events in Athena's life.

After two months, your work is going well. The building is almost finished. But one day Phidias comes to you. He looks troubled.

Turn to page **37.**

"I would like to help with a statue," you tell Phidias. Phidias has created many statues of Athena. One of his most famous is a 9-metre (30-foot) statue of the goddess. For years, it was the tallest sculpture in Athens.

Phidias answers, "I'm working on several statues right now. Some are the statues that will complete the Parthenon. I'm also working on a statue of Zeus for the temple at Olympia."

• To help with the remaining statues for the Parthenon, go to page 35

• To help with the statue of Zeus, turn to page 36

Pericles (left) and Phidias discussed plans for the Parthenon in Athens.

You are in the Parthenon, helping Phidias create several small statues for this huge temple. The work allows you to be near the new statue of Athena. The gold and ivory statue stands 11.6 metres (38 feet) tall. You think it is the most beautiful statue you have ever seen.

Your work continues for several months and is going well. But one day Phidias comes to you with a troubled look on his face.

Turn to page 37.

The statue of Zeus at Olympia was one of the Seven Wonders of the Ancient World.

You are at Olympia, helping Phidias create the statue of the god Zeus for the temple here. The magnificent statue is close to being finished. It is 12 metres (40 feet) tall and shows Zeus sitting on a huge throne. Like the statue of Athena in the Parthenon, it is made of ivory and gold.

The work is going well, but one day Phidias tells you that bad news has arrived from Athens.

"You know that Pericles and I are friends,"
Phidias says. "Pericles is a popular leader, but
like all politicians, he has enemies. Some of them
have accused me of stealing gold that was to be
used for the Parthenon's statue of Athena."

You're shocked. How could anyone accuse
Phidias of such a crime?

"You would never do that!" you tell him.

"I'm innocent," Phidias says quietly. "But if
you stay loyal to me and they find me guilty, you
risk being sent away from Athens. I'm giving
you a choice. You can stay with me and help me
prove my innocence. Or you can protect your
career and study with another sculptor. I can
recommend you to Polyclitus. You'll learn much
from him."

· To help Phidias, turn to page **38**.
· To study with Polyclitus, turn to page **55**.

Phidias has helped you a great deal. You need to help him prove his innocence.

You and Phidias meet with his accusers in the Parthenon. As you stand in front of the statue of Athena, Phidias says to you, "Peel the gold off the statue."

"I can't do that!" you reply, unable to believe your ears.

"Don't worry," he says. "I built the statue so that the gold can easily be taken off and put back on. When the gold is off, we will weigh it. That will prove there is no gold missing."

You fight to keep your hands from shaking as you peel the gold from the statue. When you are finished, the gold is weighed. It's all there! Phidias is innocent.

"I knew you didn't steal the gold," you tell Phidias later.

"Thank you for standing by me," he smiles. "But I am leaving Athens, and I don't think I'll return."

"I'll go with you," you tell him.

"No. Your life is here. If you want to continue sculpting, I will introduce you to one of Greece's best-known sculptors, Polyclitus. But when you first became my student, you said you were also interested in philosophy and medicine. If you'd like to change careers, I can introduce you to some good teachers."

· To study philosophy or medicine, turn to page **40**.

· To remain a sculptor and study with Polyclitus, turn to page **55**.

Socrates' teaching methods later became known as the Socratic Method.

You face a decision of whether to study philosophy or medicine. You have the chance to study with either Socrates or Hippocrates.

Socrates is one of the best-known Athenian philosophers. His goal is to teach his students how to find their own answers. Hippocrates also has new ideas. He is developing new ways of practising medicine.

• To study with Socrates, go to page **41**.
• To study with Hippocrates, turn to page **45**.

You decide to study with Socrates. He teaches in the agora instead of in a school. And he doesn't tell his students what to think. Instead, he keeps asking questions to help his students find an answer. As students answer the questions, they discover the answer.

Socrates remains famous throughout the city for many years. But his ideas might be too new, even in Athens. One day he is put on trial for introducing new gods and refusing to recognize Athens' gods. He is also accused of being a bad influence on the city's young men.

As a follower of Socrates, you risk getting into trouble. You might even be attacked by a mob in the agora. To avoid danger, you could break with Socrates and reject his ideas.

· To remain with Socrates, turn to page **42**.

· To break with Socrates, turn to page **57**.

Socrates' trial takes place in the agora. The 500 jurors sit on wooden benches. You stand in a crowd of people watching the trial.

Three men, Meletus, Anytus, and Lycon, have accused Socrates. Each is allowed to speak for an hour. The speeches are timed by a water clock. Water is poured into a tube inside the clock. It takes an hour for the water to run out of the tube.

After his accusers speak, Socrates gets the same amount of time. He defends himself in his three-hour speech, but he doesn't apologize.

The jury finds Socrates guilty and sentences him to death. Socrates will have to drink a poison called hemlock.

After the trial, Socrates is taken to a nearby prison. You and several of his students visit him every day.

Socrates drank hemlock, a poison that affects the central nervous system.

One day, you learn that Socrates will be put to death the next day. Early the next morning, you and the students arrive at the prison.

The jailer enters Socrates' room with a cup of hemlock. After drinking the hemlock, Socrates walks around until he says that his legs feel heavy. Then he lies on his back.

"When the poison reaches the heart, that will be the end," the jailer says.

Turn the page.

After a while, Socrates turns to a student and says, "Don't forget to pay any debts I owe."

"The debts shall be paid," the student answers. "Is there anything else?"

But Socrates doesn't answer. He is dead.

As you leave the jail, two of the students talk to you. "We're in danger if we continue studying Socrates' teachings," the first man whispers. "I've heard a mob will be waiting for us at the agora tomorrow. I'm staying at home."

"Not me," says the second student. "I'm sticking to my ideas, even if it means I might die."

The first student asks you, "What will you do tomorrow?"

· To go to the agora, turn to page 56.

· To stay at home, turn to page 57.

Hippocrates (centre) examined and closely watched his patients.

You travel to Hippocrates' medical school on the island of Kos. One day, you listen to Hippocrates talk about illness. "Many people believe sickness is punishment from the gods. But I believe that illness results from natural causes."

"The body has four fluids, or humours," he continues. "These humours are blood, black bile, yellow bile, and phlegm. When the humours are in balance, a person is healthy. When the humours are not in balance, a person gets sick. The doctor's job is to help restore the balance."

Turn the page.

Hippocrates also believes in doing complete examinations of his patients. He makes careful notes of his patients' skin colour, heartbeat, body temperature, and pains. His methods set him apart from other doctors.

You study with Hippocrates for about a year. Then the plague strikes Athens. People are dying of this horrible disease in huge numbers. Hippocrates decides to go to Athens to help fight the plague. Do you go with him or stay in Kos?

• To go to Athens, go to page 47.

• To stay in Kos, turn to page 58.

Hippocrates is doing everything he can to fight the plague. But people continue to die. Even Pericles, Athens' leader, dies from the plague. Usually, all you can do is try to keep patients comfortable and stay with them until they die.

One night, another student comes to you. "Some of the students have bought medicine that's supposed to prevent the plague," he says. "It's very powerful. I've heard a person can even die from taking it. But many of us think it's worth the risk."

"You don't know if it will work," you tell him. "And it might kill you."

47

"But what if it does work?" he replies. "I have two doses. I'm taking one. Do you want the other?"

• To take the medicine, turn to page **59**.

• To refuse the medicine, turn to page **60**.

You're a leader. You need to set a good example and try to help.

Every day, more soldiers die of the plague. But you stay well. And the Athenian army is able to keep the siege going. After three years of siege, the Potidaeans surrender and leave their city. Athenians now have the opportunity to settle in Potidaea, and you decide to stay. Soon your family joins you. You sometimes miss your old life in Athens, but you're happy in Potidaea.

THE END

To follow another path, turn to page 11.
To read the conclusion, turn to page 103.

You board a ship heading back to Athens. The journey will take several days.

The next morning, you wake up with a pounding headache. Your eyes are red and burning. Soon you are coughing up blood. You have the plague!

For a week, you lie in your bed, burning up with fever. The ship reaches Athens, but you are left alone on the boat in the harbour. No one wants to catch the plague from you. On the eighth day, you die. You never see your family or your beloved Athens again.

THE END

To follow another path, turn to page 11.
To read the conclusion, turn to page 103.

When the vote is taken, you vote no. But your side is easily defeated. Pericles stares at you with hatred. You now have a powerful enemy. And there will be war between Athens and Sparta.

At a later meeting of the Assembly, you learn just how angry Pericles is. He calls for a meeting to vote on ostracism. At this meeting, the Assembly can vote to banish any citizen from Athens for 10 years. The vote will be by a secret ballot, but you have a bad feeling that Pericles is telling people to vote to banish you.

When the ballots are counted, your fears come true. You have 10 days to leave the city. You won't be able to return for 10 years. Your vote cost you your job, your best friend, and your way of life. You're proud of standing up for your beliefs, but you're not sure it was worth it.

The Assembly used ballots to vote on ostracizing citizens of Athens.

THE END

To follow another path, turn to page 11.
To read the conclusion, turn to page 103.

You and most of the Assembly vote with Pericles. There will be war between Athens and Sparta.

As you leave the Pnyx, Pericles catches up with you. "I want you as one of my chief war advisors," he tells you. "You will be well rewarded for your loyalty." No matter what happens with the war, you are relieved that you decided to stay on Pericles' side.

THE END

To follow another path, turn to page 11.
To read the conclusion, turn to page 103.

Wooden beams were used to support columns during building construction.

You decide to work on the Propylaea. Built of white and grey marble, it has a central building and two smaller buildings.

Your job is to direct workers as they place large slabs of marble over enormous wooden beams. Your work is going well.

One morning, you climb to the roof. You stand on a beam as a crew of workers inch a heavy slab of marble into place. You move closer to make sure the slab is fitting properly.

Turn the page.

Crash! The workers drop the slab. The edge scrapes your legs.

"Help me!" you cry as you try to regain your balance on the beam. The workers leap to help you, but it's too late. You fall to your death 9 metres (30 feet) below.

THE END

To follow another path, turn to page 11.
To read the conclusion, turn to page 103.

54

You decide to study with Polyclitus in the city of Argos. Polyclitus is known for his bronze sculptures of the human body. One day, you're admiring a statue of a man holding a spear when the sculptor walks up to you.

"This statue looks so real," you tell Polyclitus. "It seems like it's about to walk across the room."

"That's because its weight is balanced on one foot," he replies. "That's how people really stand. It makes the statue look more life-like."

You are honoured to be a student of this great sculptor. One day, you hope to be as skilled as both of your famous teachers.

55

THE END

To follow another path, turn to page 11.
To read the conclusion, turn to page 103.

Socrates' student Plato (left) later became a great Athenian philosopher.

At the agora, you join several of the students. One of them is Plato, who talks about what a great teacher Socrates was.

A crowd gathers. Soon it grows into a mob of about two dozen angry men. Some shake their fists and wave clubs. Others pick up stones.

The shouting goes on, but no one makes a move to attack. After a while, you realize nothing bad will happen. As you return home, you are proud you stood up for your ideas.

THE END

To follow another path, turn to page 11.
To read the conclusion, turn to page 103.

You decide to stay away from the agora and not defend your ideas. Socrates was tried and put to death for his beliefs. You don't want the same thing to happen to you.

All morning, you listen for sounds of fighting, but none come. Then you see two of Socrates' students returning from the agora. As they pass, you listen to their conversation.

"That crowd was angry," one student says. "But all they did was yell at us."

They walk on, and you wonder if you gave up your beliefs for nothing. Then you realize that if you really believed in those ideas, you would have fought for them. Maybe one day, you'll have ideas that you'll support without question. Until then, you will keep searching.

THE END

To follow another path, turn to page 11.
To read the conclusion, turn to page 103.

You want to help Hippocrates, but you don't want to die of the plague. You decide to stay in Kos.

You continue to study with Hippocrates' sons, Thessalus and Draco, and his son-in-law, Polybus. Every day, you learn more about finding the hidden causes of diseases.

You hope to return to Athens when the plague is over and share what you've learned. But in the meantime, you're glad to be safe in Kos.

THE END

To follow another path, turn to page 11.
To read the conclusion, turn to page 103.

You swallow the medicine. It tastes awful. In the morning, you are coughing and spitting up blood. It's a sign of the plague! That night you go to bed, not knowing if you will wake up again.

The next morning, your fever and cough are gone. Within a couple of days, you are well enough to return to work.

Over the next several months, you work with Hippocrates. Finally the plague ends. You don't know if the medicine protected you from the plague, but you survived.

You look forward to learning much more from Hippocrates. Maybe one day you will be able to cure diseases like the plague.

THE END

To follow another path, turn to page 11.
To read the conclusion, turn to page 103.

Many historians today believe that the plague of Athens was typhoid fever.

"Thank you," you tell your friend, "but I don't want to take the chance on an unknown medicine." You continue to work with Hippocrates, and you stay well.

Some of the students die of the plague. You don't know if they took the medicine or not. But each time one dies, you're relieved that you refused it.

One morning you wake up with a headache and a fever. Soon you are coughing up blood. It's a sign of the plague! As the day goes on, you begin to vomit bile. Your body burns with fever, and you keep crying for water. When it's brought, you drink and drink but are still thirsty.

As you fall asleep that night, you know you won't wake up again. You look up to see Hippocrates standing over you. He whispers, "I'm sorry I could not save you." They are the last words you will ever hear.

THE END

To follow another path, turn to page 11.
To read the conclusion, turn to page 103.

Young Spartan men trained and exercised in a place called the Dromos.

CHAPTER 3

CITY OF WAR

It's a sunny spring day in Sparta. As you walk through the city, you notice many older men. They are citizens who serve in the Assembly that governs Sparta. You don't see many young Spartan men, because they are in the army. You do see Spartan women. Unlike in Athens, Spartan women have a great deal of freedom. They go where they please.

The Spartans you pass in the street all have a look of determination and discipline on their faces. They are also quiet. Spartans don't talk much. When they do talk, they say no more than they have to. That is the Spartan way.

Turn the page.

You leave the city and travel to a nearby town. Here you see merchants and craftspeople. They are perioeci, a word that means "dwellers around the city." These free people are not citizens and cannot take part in government. They work in trade and business, which Spartans are not allowed to do.

As you travel through the countryside, you see another type of people, the helots. They are the lowest class of people and are treated like slaves. They tend the land that the state gives to each Spartan family. Helots must give half the food they grow to the Spartans. They keep the rest of the food for themselves.

The three classes of people in Sparta lead very different lives. But they all play an important part in Spartan society.

‣ To live as a Spartan soldier, turn to page **66**.

‣ To see what life was like as a helot, turn to page **73**.

‣ To be a perioeci, turn to page **82**.

It is 425 BC, and you are a 35-year-old Spartan man. You have been in the army for 15 years, and you will stay in the army until you are 60. You lead a simple life filled with order and sacrifice.

Sparta has been fighting a war with Athens for six years. In war, you always fight bravely. You still remember what your mother said to you before your first battle, "Come back with your shield or on it." In other words, survive the battle or die fighting.

You live in the army barracks and eat your meals with other soldiers. Your wife and children live on your kleros, the land given to you by the state. Soldiers are officially not allowed to leave the barracks, even to see their families. But like other married soldiers, you sneak away to see your family at times.

Spartan men were expected to serve in the army for most of their lives.

You haven't seen your family in two weeks. Should you sneak away from the barracks tonight to visit them?

· To sneak away from the barracks, turn to page **68**.

· To stay in the barracks, turn to page **72**.

Stealing food was part of a young Spartan boy's military training.

You move quietly through the streets. If you are reported, you will return to the barracks in shame – not for sneaking away, but for being caught.

Suddenly you see a boy sneaking out of a house. You know that he has just stolen food from the people who live there. You also did this when you were his age.

Boys in military school are purposely not fed enough. They are expected to steal food as part of their survival training. They aren't punished for stealing, but they are punished if they're caught.

You should punish the boy for getting caught. But if you do, you risk bringing attention to yourself. Then you'll have to go back to the barracks without seeing your family.

· To punish the boy, turn to page **70**.

· To pretend you didn't see him, turn to page **88**.

You call out to the boy, and he turns and runs. You chase after him.

When you catch him, his eyes show no fear. He will take his punishment without showing his feelings, like a good Spartan.

You tell him, "You got caught." You raise your hand and hit him several times. But you don't want to really hurt the boy. You saw the courage in his eyes. You hope that your own son, who is also in military school, is as brave as this boy. Finally you say, "Go."

As you watch the boy run away, you realize that people have seen you. You have drawn attention to yourself, and now risk being reported. What should you do?

· To go back to the barracks, go to page 71.

· To continue home, turn to page 87.

You don't want to risk being reported, so you go back to the barracks. You won't see your wife, but you have been a good Spartan. You helped train a future soldier.

Your friend Kleomidas is in the barracks when you return. "There is news," he tells you. "We are going to attack the Athenian fort on the peninsula of Pylos."

Like Kleomidas, you show no feelings at the news. You nod your head and check your equipment.

You know you're expected to fight like a brave Spartan. But that means you may never see your family again. You're more likely to survive if you try to be cautious in battle.

• *To fight bravely, turn to page **89**.*

• *To be cautious, turn to page **91**.*

You stay in the barracks. You'll see your family another time.

The soldiers eat together. Your supper is barley bread and haggis. This dish is made by chopping the heart, liver, and lungs of a sheep or calf into small pieces. They are mixed with fat, onions, oatmeal, and seasonings. The entire mixture is boiled in the animal's stomach. People in other parts of Greece think Spartan food is awful. But Spartans know the purpose of food is to keep you strong, not to give you pleasure.

Halfway through supper, word arrives that you will be going into battle tomorrow. You realize being willing to die for Sparta means you may never see your family again. But you could increase your chance of survival by being cautious in battle.

• *To fight bravely, turn to page **89**.*

• *To be cautious, turn to page **91**.*

Helots grew olives and made them into olive oil.

You live in the country, a half-day's travel from Sparta. You farm a kleros that belongs to a Spartan family. You grow grain, olives, and grapes. You must give half the food you grow to the Spartan family.

Your people outnumber Spartans by about seven to one, so the Spartans don't give you a chance to overcome them. Every year, they declare war on the helots. They kill men who might become leaders or revolt against Sparta. Also, young Spartan soldiers go into the countryside. At night, they kill helots they catch outside.

Turn the page.

You're not allowed to leave your kleros and settle in a different area. Still, you know you are better off than slaves in other parts of Greece. You can't be bought or sold. You are allowed to marry and to choose your own spouse. If you have children, they are yours, not your master's. You are also allowed to have money. If you can get enough, you could pay the landowner to allow you to leave the kleros and settle somewhere else.

One day, you hear a stranger from Athens is secretly meeting with helots after dark to talk about rebellion. You want to hear what he has to say, but Spartan soldiers are hiding in the area.

· To stay at home, go to page 75.

· To go to meet the stranger, turn to page 76.

You are curious about what the stranger has to say, but you also think of your family. Freedom won't mean much to your wife and children if a Spartan kills you. You decide to stay at home.

Late that night, a neighbour knocks at your door. "A helot from a nearby kleros went to meet the stranger," he tells you. "On the way home, a Spartan killed him."

You are relieved you stayed at home. But as you fall asleep that night, you dream of freedom.

One day, amazing news comes from Sparta. Spartan leaders want 2,000 helots to fight with the Spartan army. The helots will be given their freedom in return. This is the chance you've been waiting for. Yet you fear it could be a Spartan trick.

· To stay at home, turn to page **80**.
· To go to Sparta, turn to page **94**.

You arrive at the meeting and find four others there. One is the stranger from Athens.

"The time is right to rebel against Sparta," the stranger says. "I'm gathering helots who are willing to fight."

"I remember stories of the last helot rebellion, almost 40 years ago," says an old man. "The Spartans laid siege to the rebels' mountain stronghold but couldn't defeat them. The Spartans finally gave the rebels their freedom if they promised to leave Laconia and never return."

"You see?" the stranger adds. "Sparta doesn't always win. And soon Sparta will be at war with Athens. The Spartans will have to fight Athenians as well as helots."

After the meeting ends, you leave one by one, creeping into the darkness. You take a shortcut through a field.

Suddenly a young Spartan soldier appears in your path. You know that he plans to kill you.

• To run away, turn to page **78**.
• To fight the Spartan, turn to page **93**.

You turn and dash into the darkness. You hear the soldier's footsteps right behind you. You have one advantage. You have worked these fields for years and know every inch of the ground.

Unlike this soldier, the Spartans who hunted helots were not yet fully fledged warriors.

The soldier is gaining on you. You run faster. Suddenly you come to a wide ditch. You spring into the air and land on the other side. You hear a thump as the Spartan hits the ground. He didn't see the ditch.

You keep running. Soon the only sound you hear is the pounding of your heart. A few minutes later, you arrive at your house. You decide that joining the rebellion is too dangerous. You may not be free, but at least you're alive.

One day, news comes from Sparta. Sparta has been fighting a war with Athens for the last six years. The Spartans will set free 2,000 helots who agree to fight for Sparta. You've been waiting for this chance. But what if it's a trick?

• *To stay at home, turn to page* **80**.

• *To go to Sparta, turn to page* **94**.

You are sure that this offer is a Spartan trick. Yet as you watch other helots leave, you wonder if you're making the right decision.

One day, a traveller stops by your house and asks for a drink of water. "The helots in Sparta are being treated well," he tells you. "They can go anywhere they please. They are even allowed to go to the temples."

Have you made a huge mistake?

But weeks later, another traveller tells you something very different. "All the helots who went to Sparta have disappeared. No one knows what happened to them. Some people say that the Spartans killed them all." That night you dream of fighting Sparta for your freedom.

In 432 BC, the Peloponnesian League met to consider war with Athens. The war began the next year.

One day, news comes that 420 Spartan soldiers are trapped on the island of Sphacteria after the Battle of Pylos. Sparta wants helots to risk their lives to bring supplies to the trapped soldiers. Helots who succeed will be freed. You remember what happened the last time the Spartans offered freedom. Is this another trick?

· To go to Sphacteria, turn to page **96**.

· To stay at home, turn to page **97**.

You are a member of the perioeci, the free people who live in the Laconia territory outside Sparta. Your people have settled about 80 small towns surrounding the city.

When the Spartans conquered Laconia hundreds of years ago, your people weren't made slaves, like the helots. Perioeci have a special role in Spartan society. Spartans are not allowed to work in business, and helots can only farm. Perioeci are the craftspeople and business owners. They make pots, spin wool, and weave clothing.

Your people don't have unlimited rights. Perioeci can't marry Spartans or participate in the government. You pay taxes to Sparta and must serve in the army if called.

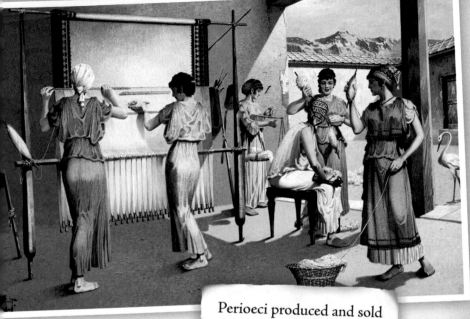

Perioeci produced and sold cloth and other items.

But in some ways you have more freedom than Spartan citizens do. You can travel to other cities without permission. You can own land. You wear clothes that are warmer than Spartans' clothing. You are allowed to own gold and silver. Some perioeci have even become rich.

Turn the page.

Perioeci are given these freedoms because Sparta doesn't fear them. When the helots rebelled almost 40 years ago, only two perioeci towns joined them. The other towns remained loyal to Sparta. You wish for more rights, but you realize your people don't have the weapons or training to defeat the Spartans.

One day, you receive orders to join the Spartan army. You're not sure you are willing to die for Sparta. But if you don't join the army, you'll have to leave the city.

· To join the army, go to page **85**.

· To refuse, turn to page **101**.

Triremes had three rows of oars.

You are aboard a Spartan ship called a trireme, attacking the Athenians on the peninsula of Pylos. The Spartans have 43 triremes, but the battle isn't going well for them. The water is rough and the coast is rocky. Some captains are hesitating to unload their soldiers. They're afraid of crashing the ships on the rocks.

Turn the page.

Finally one captain, Brasidas, takes control of the situation. "Push forward!" he yells at the other captains. "What use is saving your ship if we lose the battle?"

Brasidas orders his crew to run up the trireme on land. Inspired by Brasidas, your captain does the same thing. As your boat hits the shore, you leap out to face the Athenians.

The surf pounds against you, and the rocks underfoot are slippery. The Spartans outnumber the Athenians, but your men are not coming ashore quickly enough. There is still time to run away. What will you do?

· To keep fighting, turn to page **98**.

· To turn back, turn to page **100**.

You don't believe the people who saw you will report you. Soon, you reach your kleros. When you and your wife see each other, neither of you shows emotion. That is not the Spartan way. Your wife asks, "What is happening with the war?"

"Athens won't give up," you answer. "I may be heading into battle soon."

As you get ready to leave, there is a knock at the door. Two of your fellow soldiers are standing there. "You've been caught outside the barracks," one of them tells you. "We're to bring you back to be punished."

You hang your head, but you don't protest. You know you deserve the severe beating you'll receive back at the barracks. Next time, you will be more careful.

THE END

To follow another path, turn to 11.
To read the conclusion, turn to page 103.

The boy freezes, waiting to see what you will do. Only a few seconds go by, but it seems much longer. Then you continue on your way, pretending you didn't see the boy. He runs off in the other direction.

Suddenly you realize that you were wrong to pretend you didn't see the boy. You should have punished him to make him stronger. You haven't been a good Spartan. You don't deserve to see your family. You start back to the barracks.

As you walk towards the barracks, you hear a hissing sound. A snake on the ground darts out and bites your foot. As you sink to the ground, you realize that you're dying from the bite. The gods must be punishing you for being a bad Spartan. As you close your eyes, you hope they will show mercy on you in the afterlife.

THE END

To follow another path, turn to page 11.
To read the conclusion, turn to page 103.

Most sea battles involved ramming triremes into each other.

You are aboard one of 43 Spartan triremes. These ships have three rows of oars on each side. You and your fellow soldiers are about to attack the military base on Pylos.

The rocky landing point is difficult to reach. Some captains are hanging back to avoid wrecking their ships on the rocks.

"Push forward!" Brasidas, your captain, yells at them. "Sacrifice your boats for Sparta if that's what it takes!"

Turn the page.

You and the other soldiers obey Brasidas and run your boat onto the shore. There, a large number of Athenian soldiers stand ready to attack. Brasidas is about to jump out when he is badly wounded. Still alive, he falls into the boat as his shield slips into the sea.

Spurred on by Brasidas' courage, you leap out of the boat. Two enemy soldiers thrust at you with spears. Two more lunge at you with swords. You fight bravely, but there are too many blades to dodge. An enemy sword finds its target in your chest. You fall to the ground, your hands stained with your own blood. Your last thought is that you are proud to have given your life for Sparta.

THE END

To follow another path, turn to page 11.
To read the conclusion, turn to page 103.

The Spartan army has sailed to the rocky peninsula of Pylos. A force of Athenian soldiers waits for you on the beach.

You leap onto the shore along with your fellow soldiers. But instead of heading into the thick of the battle, you hang back. There are fewer soldiers to fight here. You manage to kill or wound a few enemy soldiers, but not as many as you usually do.

Your side has many more soldiers. But the Athenians hold you off for more than a day. Finally your commanders order you to stop fighting. They plan a siege. Spartan ships will surround Pylos and prevent any ships or supplies from reaching the enemy soldiers.

As you're getting ready for the siege, you hear a shout from a lookout. "Athenian ships are coming! At least 50 of them! Block the harbour!"

Turn the page.

Spartan soldiers fought Athens' strong navy during the Peloponnesian War.

You and the other soldiers rush to the harbour, but it's too late. The reinforcements help Athens win the battle.

You hang your head in shame. If you had only fought harder, Sparta might have won the battle before the ships arrived. You know you've failed as a Spartan.

THE END

To follow another path, turn to page 11.
To read the conclusion, turn to page 103.

The Spartan is armed only with a knife. You pick up a sharp branch lying on the ground. It's longer than the Spartan's knife, and you think you can defend yourself with it. The two of you circle each other.

Suddenly the Spartan leaps on you. He knocks the branch out of your hand and thrusts his knife at your throat. As the knife flashes in the moonlight, you know that in seconds you will be dead. But death will finally free you from a life of hard work and fear. Then the knife plunges down, and everything goes dark.

93

THE END

To follow another path, turn to page 11.
To read the conclusion, turn to page 103.

You are in Sparta with about 2,000 other helots. You are allowed to go anywhere you please. You are even allowed to go to the temples. For the first time, you know what it is like to be free.

But as the days pass, something strange happens. Each day, you see fewer and fewer helots. No one seems to know what has happened to those who have disappeared.

The more you think about it, the more worried you become. That night, you decide to leave Sparta at dawn.

As you fall asleep, you hear a rustling noise. Then you feel the cold steel of a Spartan blade against your chest. You open your eyes and see a Spartan soldier at the other end of the sword.

Now you understand what happened to the helots who disappeared. This offer of freedom was a Spartan trick.

Your last thought is, "The Spartans will never give us a chance to become strong."

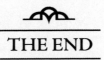

THE END

To follow another path, turn to page 11.
To read the conclusion, turn to page 103.

It is night, and you are crouched in a small boat loaded with food for the soldiers trapped on Sphacteria. If you live through this, you will be free. But Athenian ships surround the island. If Athenian soldiers catch you, they will kill you.

A storm is brewing. It isn't safe to be on the water, but this is the best time to get past the Athenian ships.

Tonight you are lucky. The wind carries your boat quickly to the island. When the boat lands, Spartan soldiers rush out of the darkness and unload the precious supplies.

As you sail away from the island, you think about the grateful look on the soldiers' faces when they saw the food. This was no Spartan trick. Soon you will be a free man.

THE END

To follow another path, turn to page 11.
To read the conclusion, turn to page 103.

You won't risk your life for Sparta. If Athenians catch the helots, they will kill them.

In the coming days, you wonder if you made the right decision. Each day is the same as you toil in the fields and wait for news.

Finally the news comes. The Spartans on Sphacteria surrendered. Your first reaction is amazement. No one thought Spartans would surrender. Perhaps they are not as brave as everyone thinks.

You ask about the helots who went to Sphacteria. Several were killed. But the ones who lived were set free. Had you gone, you might have won your freedom. But you might have died in the attempt. You aren't free, but at least you're still alive.

THE END

To follow another path, turn to page 11.
To read the conclusion, turn to page 103.

Spartan officer Brasidas (centre) was wounded at Pylos but survived.

The Athenians are well prepared for this attack. You're sloshing through the water. Your armour weighs you down. Arrows fall around you. Behind you, Spartan soldiers fall dead in the sea. Ships crash into the rocks.

Someone calls out, "Brasidas has fallen!" You turn and see men in Brasidas' boat trying to help their wounded captain. His shield falls into the water. An Athenian soldier scoops it up, holding it in the air as a war trophy.

Now two Athenians are coming at you. There is no turning back. You lunge forward and fight with all your might. But as a shrill whistle fills the air, arrows rain down on you. Several of them hit their targets. You stumble, fall into the surf, and die. Your last thought is, "I died for nothing."

99

THE END

To follow another path, turn to page 11.
To read the conclusion, turn to page 103.

Quickly, you decide to try to get back to your ship. Behind you, Spartan soldiers lie dead in the water. Ships crash into the rocks. The Athenians are fighting fiercely, and most of your soldiers are still in their boats. You realize it's hopeless.

You slowly move back as you dodge thrusting spears and whistling arrows. You don't think you'll make it, but you finally reach your ship. Soldiers in the ship are fighting off the Athenians. As they push the ship off shore, you jump in.

Exhausted, you stare at the dead bodies floating in the surf. The Spartan army has lost, but you are still alive. You hope that the next battle will go better for your army.

THE END

To follow another path, turn to page 11.
To read the conclusion, turn to page 103.

You won't fight for Sparta. You decide to go to the city-state of Thebes in the region of Boeotia. Sparta and Thebes have not always been on friendly terms, but now Thebes is an ally of Sparta. You hope you will be welcome in Thebes.

Perioeci are free to travel, so your visit to Thebes won't be unusual. You will say you are travelling on business. But you have to be careful. If the Thebans learn you left Laconia to avoid joining the Spartan army, they might arrest you.

After several days, you arrive in Thebes. As you walk through the city's bustling market, you believe you will be able to make a new life here. At last, you are truly free.

THE END

To follow another path, turn to page 11.
To read the conclusion, turn to page 103.

Musicians played as buildings of Athens were pulled down after the Peloponnesian War.

CHAPTER 4

AFTER THE GOLDEN AGE

Athens and Sparta went to war in 431 BC. This conflict is called the Peloponnesian War. During the first year of the war, Athenians stopped work on the Propylaea. This grand building was to be the gateway to the city's acropolis. It was never finished.

The Peloponnesian War was a turning point in ancient Greek history. At first, Athens seemed to have the advantage. But the plague that struck Athens in 430 BC changed everything. Many historians believe that this disease was typhoid fever. At least one-third of Athenians died, including the city's leader, Pericles.

103

Even so, Athens continued to fight for 26 more years. After Athens surrendered in 404 BC, Sparta tore down Athens' walls and set up its own government to rule the city.

The Greek city-states continued to fight one another and became weaker as a result. Meanwhile Macedonia, a kingdom to the north, became stronger. In 338 BC, the Macedonians scored a major military victory against Greece. As a result, Greece lost much of its independence.

In 336 BC, Alexander the Great became the king of Macedonia. His empire eventually stretched from Greece to India. The time following Alexander's death in 323 BC is called the Hellenistic Age. During this time, Greek philosophy, literature, politics, religion, art, and law spread from Africa to India. The Hellenistic Age lasted until 146 BC, when the Romans took control of Greece.

The ancient Greeks laid the foundations of western civilization. Modern democracies are built on Greek beliefs in government by the people, trial by jury, and equality. Greeks introduced forms of literature that include comedy and tragedy. Today, doctors take an oath based on the teachings of Hippocrates. Greek ideas about art and architecture continue to inspire modern artists.

We haven't learned all there is to know about ancient Greece. Archeologists are still discovering ruins. Great minds of today are still studying the ideas of the ancient Greek philosophers. In many ways, this fascinating civilization is very much alive in our modern world.

Time line

900–700 BC – Sparta takes control of the people in regions around it. Some people are made slaves and become helots. Others lose their political rights but are allowed to remain free. They become perioeci.

550–371 BC – Sparta is at the height of its power.

480 BC – Persia defeats Greek city-states at the Battle of Thermopylae.

479 BC – The Greeks defeat the Persians at the Battle of Plataea and drive them out of Greece.

464 BC – The most successful helot rebellion against Sparta begins.

461 BC – Pericles begins to dominate politics in Athens.

461–404 BC – The Golden Age of Athens.

432 BC – The siege of Potidaea begins. The Battle of Sybota is fought.

431 BC – The Peloponnesian War begins.

430 BC – The plague strikes Athens.

429 BC – Pericles dies of the plague.

425 BC – Spartans kill 2,000 helots who volunteer as soldiers. The Battle of Pylos is fought, followed by the Battle of Sphacteria.

404 BC – Sparta wins the Peloponnesian War and becomes the dominant city-state in Greece.

399 BC – Socrates is tried and sentenced to death.

371 BC – Thebes defeats Sparta at the Battle of Leuctra. Thebes becomes the dominant city-state in Greece.

338 BC – Greece loses much of its independence to Macedonia.

323–146 BC – During the Hellenistic Age, Greek culture dominates the eastern Mediterranean and Middle Eastern parts of the world.

146 BC – The Romans take control of Greece.

OTHER PATHS TO EXPLORE

In this book, you've seen how the events surrounding ancient Greece look different from two points of view.

Perspectives on history are as varied as the people who lived it. You can explore other paths on your own to learn more about what happened. Seeing history from many points of view is an important part of understanding it.

Here are some ideas for other ancient Greece points of view to explore:

+ The Olympic Games were an important part of Greek culture. What was it like to be an athlete or a spectator at the games?

+ Religion was important in ancient Greece. What was it like to be a storyteller who shared tales about gods and goddesses?

+ Some of the world's most famous plays were written in ancient Greece. What was it like to be a playwright during this time?

READ MORE

100 Facts: Ancient Greece, Fiona Macdonald (Miles Kelly Publishing, 2009)

Ancient Greece, Jane, Kevin & Priscilla Wood (Collins, 2012)

Ancient Greece (Eyewitness Project Books) (DK Publishing, 2014)

Men, Women and Children: In Ancient Greece, Colin Hyson (Wayland, 2007)

INTERNET SITES

Visit these sites to find out more about life in Ancient Greece:

www.bbc.co.uk/schools/primaryhistory/ancient_greeks/

www.childrensuniversity.manchester.ac.uk/interactives/history/greece/

www.ngkids.co.uk/did-you-know/10-facts-about-the-Ancient-Greeks

GLOSSARY

aristocrat – wealthy person in ancient Greece

helot – member of the lowest class in Sparta

hoplite – heavily armed infantry soldier of ancient Greece

kleros – land given to a Spartan citizen by the state

ostracism – method of temporarily banishing people in ancient Greece

perioeci – people in ancient Laconia who were conquered by Sparta but not made slaves

philosopher – person who studies truth, wisdom, the nature of reality, and knowledge

plague – deadly disease that spreads quickly

siege – attack designed to surround a place and cut it off from supplies or help

trireme – ship with oars placed on three levels

BIBLIOGRAPHY

Cartledge, Paul. *Sparta and Lakonia: A Regional History, 1300–362 BC.* London: Routledge & Kegan Paul, 1979.

Cartledge, Paul. *Spartan Reflections.* Berkeley, Calif.: University of California Press, 2001.

Herodotus. *The History of Herodotus.* http://classics.mit.edu/Herodotus/history.1.i.html

Jones, A. H. M. *Sparta.* Oxford, U.K.: Blackwell and Mott, 1967.

Powell, Anton. *Athens and Sparta: Constructing Greek Political and Social History from 478 BC.* Portland, Ore.: Areopagitica Press, 1988.

Roberts, Jennifer T., and Tracy Barrett. *The Ancient Greek World.* Oxford, U.K.: Oxford University Press, 2004.

Robinson, C. E. *Everyday Life in Ancient Greece.* New York: AMS Press, 1977.

Thucydides. *History Of The Peloponnesian War.* http://www.acs.ucalgary.ca/~vandersp/Courses/texts/thucydi1.html

Webster, T. B. L. *Everyday Life in Classical Athens.* New York: Putnam, 1969.

INDEX